Wildlife Heroes

The Story of Joy and George Adamson

By Jack L. Roberts

Curious Kids Press

Palm Springs, CA 92264

Wildlife Heroes

The Story of Joy and George Adamson

E-book edition © 2014

Print Edition © 2017

Front Cover: Photo © Copyright Elsa Conservation Trust.

Used by permission.

Interior Page Design and Composition: Michael Owens

"Who will now care for the animals,
for they cannot look after themselves?
Are there young men and women
who are willing to take on this charge?
Who will raise their voices,
when mine is carried away on the wind,
to plead their case?"
— George Adamson, 1906-1989

Table of Contents

Joy and George Adamson with Elsa.

Prologue

Who Were Joy and George Adamson?

*"Joy and George together completely
transformed the way the world felt about
conservation, about keeping animals in captivity,
and about looking after the environment."*

— Tony Fitzjohn

JOY AND GEORGE ADAMSON were two of the most famous wildlife **conservationists** in the world. They did something no one else had ever done. They did something no one believed *could* be done. What was that?

Joe and George walking in the African Bush.

They raised a lion cub as a pet. They named her Elsa. When Elsa grew up, they helped her learn to survive in the **African bush** in Kenya, a country in Africa.

Most people said Elsa would not survive. They said she didn't know how to hunt for food on her own. She didn't know how to protect itself. Many experts also said Elsa wouldn't be accepted by other lions. She had too many human smells.

But Joy and George proved those people wrong. It wasn't easy. It took much longer than they thought it would to get Elsa used to living on her own in the wild. But, in the end, they succeeded. Elsa mated in the wild. She produced her own litter of cubs.

Later Joy wrote a book about their adventures. She called it *Born Free*. It told about the fun of raising Elsa as a pet. It told about how difficult it was to return Elsa to the wild.

But Joy and George did something else just as important. They made the world aware of the need to protect wild animals. They fought against **poachers**. They fought against the random killing of wild animals just for the "fun" of it.

Joy and George spent nearly 40 years of their adult lives in the African bush. It wasn't always easy. They were shot at by poachers; they were snapped at by crocodiles. They were charged by rhinos; they were spit at by cobras. They were even attacked by the very lions they raised and loved.

But Joy and George never gave up. When they first arrived in Kenya, there was not a single national park where wildlife was protected.

Today, there are 22 **National Parks** in Kenya and 28 **National Reserves** — thanks in large part to the work that Joy and George Adamson did to bring awareness to African wildlife.

This, then, is their story — the story of two wild life heroes.

Think About It

1. Many people did not think that a lion raised as a pet could be released back into the bush. Why? Give three reasons the text says.

2. Why do you think the author calls Joy and George Adamson "wildlife heroes"? Base your answer on information in the text.

Chapter 1

Young Joy Adamson

"I felt like a murderess and vowed never again to shoot for sport. I determined to devote my life to saving wild animals."

— Joy Adamson

JOY ADAMSON WAS BORN Friederike Victoria Gessner in Austria on January 20, 1910. She was one of three daughters of a very wealthy family.

As a young girl, Joy had everything any young girl could want. She would go skiing in the winter and play at her grandmother's estate in the summer.

Friederike Victoria Gessner (Joy Adamson)

When she was fifteen, she had an experience that changed her life forever. She was walking on the estate with the **gameskeeper**. Suddenly, he spotted a deer. He handed his rifle to Joy and told her to shoot. Without thinking, she did!

Instantly, she felt remorse (or extreme sadness). She couldn't believe she had shot such a beautiful animal just for the fun of it. She vowed that she would never shoot another wild animal for sport as long as she lived. She also determined then and there to devote her life to saving wild animals.

When Joy was in her early twenties, she met a young man called Ziebel. After only three weeks, Ziebel proposed. Shortly after that, on March 28, 1935, they were married. Joy was 25 years old.

Ziebel was rich. So in the summer they traveled; in the winter they skied. At the same time, they talked about where they might want to settle down.

Two years later, Ziebel suggested they might live in Africa. But he wanted Joy to go there first to see if she liked it. He planned so join her later.

So on May 12, 1937, Joy sailed for Africa. On her voyage, Joy met a man named Peter Bally. He was a **botanist**. He was going to Africa to study and write about Africa plants.

Joy and Peter hit it off immediately. They had a shipboard romance. He is the first person to call her "Joy." Was it because she brought him great joy?

The two spent a great deal of time together in Africa. Finally, when Joy returned to Europe, she told Ziebel she wanted a divorce. She wanted to marry Peter.

The divorce was granted. And in March 1938 Joy sailed for Africa once again. In April Joy and Peter were married.

For the next several years Joy and Peter traveled throughout Kenya. He studied and wrote about plants. She drew detailed pictures of the plants and flowers. She discovered she was an excellent artist. Later, she painted scenes from African tribal life.

In 1942, Joy and Peter went to a Christmas party at a friend's house near Nairobi, the capital of Kenya. There, she met a man named George Adamson. He was a **game warden** in Africa.

For George, it was love at first sight. "I decided I could not live without her," he later said.

Joy may have had the same feeling. George was tall, dark, and handsome with bold blue eyes and blond hair.

George invited Joy and her husband Peter to join him on a camel **safari**. During that safari, Joy fell in love. "George was opening up a new world to me with his stories of wild animals."

At the same time, George discovered many things he loved about this beautiful young woman. For one, she could also keep up with him. She could look after herself in the bush. She could walk as far as he could. She could endure the hardship of living in the bush. And, perhaps most importantly, she cared as much about the animals as he did.

By the time the safari was over, Joy knew what she had to do. She asked Peter for a divorce. He agreed. And, on January 17, 1944, Joy and George were married. It was beginning of a nearly 40-year relationship in the heart of the African bush.

Think About It

1. The text says that as a young girl Joy shot a deer. She then "vowed" never to shoot another wild animal for sport. Based on the text, what does it mean to make a vow?

2. The text says Joy and Peter Bally "hit it off." What can you conclude is the meaning of the phrase "hit it off"?

3. Based on the text, what are three adjectives that you think best describe Joy. Choose your adjectives based on what the text says about Joy and what you can guess about her.

Kenya At-a-Glance

Official Name: Republic of Kenya

Population: 45,010,056 as of 2014 (about 7 million more than the state of California)

Area: 224,081 square miles (580,367 square kilometers); slightly smaller than the state of Texas.

Capital: Nairobi

Languages: Swahili, English, other native languages

Climate: Tropical along coast; temperate inland

Chapter 2
George Adamson: Father of Lions

GEORGE ADAMSON DIDN'T PLAN to become a game warden in Africa. In fact, as a young man, George didn't know what he wanted to do.

George was born in British India on February 3, 1906. A year later his parents gave him a baby brother named Terence. The two young boys would remain close throughout their lives.

George Adamson

After George graduated from boarding school, he went to Kenya. His parents had bought a small coffee farm near Nairobi.

At first, George worked on the coffee farm. But he became restless. He wanted more excitement and adventure in his life.

So for the next few years, he worked at a variety of odd jobs. He prospected for gold. He sold insurance. He hunted buffalo. He led safaris in Kenya.

Finally, in 1938 at the age of 32, George joined Kenya's Game Department as a game warden. From the very first day he knew this was a job he could love. And it is one he kept for the next 23 years.

George's job as game warden involved many things. He dealt with poachers; he helped settle tribal fights and disagreements; he worked to control various diseases throughout the region.

At the end of 1942, George met a young woman named Joy Bally. He fell in love instantly! And, in 1944, after her divorce, the two were married.

When Joy and George first settled in Kenya, wildlife was in abundance. But gradually things began to change. The government did not seem to care much about the wildlife in Kenya.

People at that time killed wild animals for different reasons. Often, they killed wild animals for no reason at all! Humans were the most dangerous **predators** of wild animals.

Farmers hated the wild animals. Cheetahs would sometimes attack and kill a farmer's cattle; elephants would destroy their crops. Sometimes the farmers would hunt down the animals and kill them — just to get even.

Young men often killed lions and other wild animals just for fun. They thought it showed how brave they were.

Poachers hunted and killed wild animals for the money they could make. They hunted and killed tigers for their skins or for **medicinal** purposes.

They hunted and killed elephants for their ivory tusks. In some Asian nations an elephant's ivory tusks were worth more than gold.

They hunted and killed rhinoceroses for their horns. A rhino's horn could be worth as much as a half million dollars!

There were also Big Game hunters. They came from all over the world. They enjoyed the "sport" of killing these animals.

Joy and George Adamson worked hard to stop poaching. They work hard to create awareness about the importance of protecting wild animals. They wanted to protect wild animals for future generations.

Think About It

1. The text says "Humans are the most dangerous predators of wild animals." Based on the text, what can you conclude is the meaning of the word predator?

2. Name three reasons the text says that people often kill wild animals.

Poachers Kill Beloved Elephant

IN JUNE 2014, one of Kenya's largest and most beloved elephants was killed — by poisoned darts!

The elephant's name was Satao. He lived in Tsavo East National Park in Kenya. And he was known for his massive tusks. They were so big they touched the ground.

Poachers wanted Satao's tusks. And they were determined to get them. So they tracked Satao using GPS and mobile phones.

Finally, they found him. And killed him!

"A great life lost," said a Kenya conservationist, "so that someone far away can have a trinket on their mantelpiece."

Today, it is illegal to kill an elephant in Africa. Yet, that hasn't stopped poachers. In 2011 poaching hit the highest level in decades. As long as people buy ivory souvenirs like jewelry, or chopsticks or religious figurines, poachers will continue to track and kill elephants — like Satao!

Chapter 3
Elsa: An Ambassador for Her Kind

"A lion deserves to be free to hunt and to choose its own prey; to look for and find its own mate; to fight for and hold its own territory; and to die where it was born — in the wild. It should have the same rights as we have."

— George Adamson

IN FEBRUARY 1956 a local tribesman in Kenya was killed by a man-eating lion. As game warden of the area, it was George's job to find the lion and kill it.

He had gone out one morning with another warden looking for the man-eating lion. All of a sudden a lioness charged at them. George instinctively raised his rifle and fired!

Only afterward did George discover why the lioness had charged them. She was trying to protect her three cubs. George rescued the cubs and brought them back to camp.

When Joy saw the three cubs, she immediately picked them up and cuddled them in her arms. "Little did I know," Joy later wrote, "that on that morning my whole life would be changed forever."

All of the cubs were female. Each had its own personality, even at this young age. Joy described the littlest one as the "weakling in size, but the pluckiest in spirit." Joy named her Elsa.

For a while, Joy and George kept the three cubs with them. They let them run free. But, eventually, they decided to send two of the cubs to a zoo in Holland.

Joy with Elsa and her sisters.

Joy and George kept Elsa. They took her with them on safaris. Elsa loved to ride on the roof of the old Land Rover. They taught her to eat from their hands. They even let her sleep in their bed. Elsa loved to fall asleep, sucking Joy's thumb. Often she would wake them up by licking their face with her rough tongue.

During this time, as Elsa grew, the bond between Joy and Elsa also grew. "As long as she was with us and knew herself to be loved and secure, she was happy," says Joy.

By the time Elsa was almost two years old, she had grown large and strong. She was also becoming more independent, much like a young teenager. Sometimes after an evening walk she refused to return home. Instead, she stayed out in the bush.

Once when she refused to come home Joy and George went looking for her. They found her sitting on a rock in the moonlight. Not too far away were a lion and two lionesses. They were calling to her.

At the same time Joy and George called Elsa to come to them. Elsa didn't move. She didn't know what to do. Should she go with her own kind? Or should she return to her foster parents who loved her?

Finally, the other lions slowly sauntered off. For a moment it looked like Elsa was going to follow them. But, almost reluctantly, she turned back and followed Joy and George home to safety.

Think About It

1. What happened between Joy and Elsa? Why?

2. Why couldn't Elsa continue to live with Joy and George?

3. Conduct a short research project about the Big Cats of Africa. Compare and contrast their size, habitat, behavior, and other characteristics.

The Big Cats of East Africa

THE TIGER, LION, JAGUAR, AND LEOPARD are often called the Big Cats of Africa.

Lions are unique among the Big Cats in one special way. They are the only cats that live and hunt in groups. A group or "pride" usually consists of a number of related females and a few unrelated males.

Unlike other Big Cats, lions are also affectionate. They form strong social bonds. They enjoy head rubbing, licking, and purring.

Lions have some natural enemies, like the buffalo or elephant. But the biggest threat to lions comes from human beings who hunt and kill lions. Today, lions are considered "vulnerable" to extinction. That means one day there may no longer be any lions.

Chapter 4
Return to the Wild

"Sitting there with Elsa close to me, I felt as though I were on the doorstep of paradise: man and beast in trusting harmony."

— Joy Adamson

JOY AND GEORGE WERE FACED with a difficult decision. Elsa was now too big to continue living with them. Should they send Elsa to a zoo? Or should they release her (let her go) back into the wild? Neither choice would be easy. For Joy, for George, or for Elsa!

Joy hated the thought of sending Elsa to a zoo. Elsa had been born free. Joy wanted her to live free.

Joy and Elsa relaxing in the bush.

So Joy and George decided to help Elsa develop her **natural born instincts**. They put a plan together to return Elsa to the wild.

At first, they thought it would take only two or three weeks. They would take Elsa to a new area that was known to have lots of other lions.

During the first week, they would walk around this new area with Elsa. They would help her get used to her new surroundings.

The second week they would leave Elsa overnight in the bush. Each morning they would return to visit and feed her.

Gradually, they would reduce the food they gave her. They hoped this would encourage Elsa to look for her own food. In order to survive in the wild, she had to learn to kill for herself.

Finally, they would leave Elsa alone for several days at a time. They hoped that when they returned they would find Elsa sitting by a **carcass** that she had killed and eaten.

At least, that was the plan. But that's not what happened. Not by a long shot!

Each time Joy and George returned they found Elsa in the same spot — exactly where they left her! She was always hungry. Sometimes she was shivering with cold. Joy could tell she was unhappy.

But as soon as she saw Joy and George, guess what happened. Elsa was full of affection. "She was overjoyed to see us, desperate to stay with us," says Joy. "She sucked my thumbs frantically to make sure that everything was all right between us."

In the end it took almost two years to get Elsa used to living on her own in the bush. During that time, Joy and George kept a detailed record of her progress. It was slow.

Finally, one morning in 1959 Joy and George were out walking with Elsa. George spotted a waterbuck. He raised his gun, and shot it. At the same moment, Elsa jumped at the waterbuck's throat.

"It was her first experience of killing a large animal," Joy later said. "We now saw that she knew the vital spot by instinct." She knew how to kill her **prey** quickly.

Joy and George were overjoyed. It meant that Elsa could survive in the bush on her own. It meant she could live free.

Think About It

1. Present an argument in favor of (or opposed to) the returning Elsa to the wild or sending her to a zoo. Use appropriate facts from the text in your argument.

2. Explain the plan that Joy and George had for returning Elsa to the wild. Refer to details and examples in the text.

Chapter 5
The Death of Elsa

"Reading about Elsa, people seemed to realize how lovable [wild animals] could be if we didn't treat them as inferior and stupid."

— Joy Adamson

JOY AND GEORGE'S EXPERIMENT was a success! Elsa survived very well in the wild. She soon mated with a wild lion. She gave birth to three cubs.

For the first six weeks, Elsa kept her cubs hidden from Joy and George. Then, slowly she brought each one across a six-foot deep river close to the camp. She wanted to introduce them to their "grandparents."

In January 1961 Joy left for a short business trip to Nairobi. When she left, Elsa was fine.

But soon George noticed that something was wrong. Elsa seemed very sick. She was weak. Her breathing seemed painful. She was too ill to even pay attention to her cubs.

So George spent the night with her. He lay by her side. Even though Elsa was very weak, she would rub her face against his. It was her way of showing affection.

The next morning Elsa seemed to be doing a little better. George went about his usual morning routine. Later that day he went into his tent. Elsa was there.

George lay down beside her. He was dozing off. "Suddenly," George wrote, "she got up. She quickly walked to the front of the tent and collapsed." Elsa was gone!

Elsa died from what was believed to be a tick disease. George buried her in a grave at Meru National Park where they lived. In her honor, he then fired his rifle 20 times over her grave.

When Joy heard the news about Elsa, she was heartbroken. "With Elsa's death," she said, "a vital part of my life died too."

Joy and George became guardians of Elsa's cubs. The cubs were not yet quite old enough to hunt and survive on their own in the wild.

Eventually, Joy and George took them to the Serengeti National Park in Tanzania. They were returned to the wild to live free.

During this time, Joy wrote two more books about their adventures in raising the cubs and about Elsa's death. One book was called *Living Free: The Story of Elsa and Her Cubs*. The other was *Forever Free: Elsa's Pride*.

In 1966 a movie was made based on Joy's first book about Elsa, *Born Free*. It became a huge hit.

Joy and George served as advisers to the movie. Two half-grown lion cubs had major roles in the movie. One was named Boy; the other Girl. George's job was to train them for their roles in the movie. Boy became one of George's favorite lions.

By now, Joy's books about Elsa had become best-sellers. Joy, George, and Elsa were famous throughout the world. Everyone wanted to know more about Elsa and about Joy and George's life in the bush.

Joy loved it. She went on dozens of speaking tours to dozens of countries. She spoke about Elsa and the importance of wildlife **preservation**.

Joy also started an organization called the Elsa Wild Animal Appeal. Its goal was to raise money to set up animal reserves in Kenya.

Meanwhile, George hated all the attention. He just wanted to be left alone to work with his lions. Slowly, he and Joy were drifting apart.

Think About It

1. The text says that when Elsa died a "vital" part of Joy's life died too. Based on the text, what does *vital* mean?

2. Explain how Joy and George's life changed after the release of the movie *Born Free*.

Chapter 6
A Perfect Place to Raise Lions

"Animals give us something we cannot get from our own kind."

— Joy Adamson

AFTER THE MOVIE WAS MADE, Joy and George returned to their camp in Meru National Park. They brought with them a small **pride** from the film, including Boy and Girl. They planned to help the young lions return to the wild.

Joy also brought a young cheetah cub named Pippa to Meru as well. She had been given Pippa to **rehabilitate** into the wild shortly before filming was completed.

Joy with her cheetah Pippa.

Joy's work with Pippa was successful, just like it was with Elsa. Pippa returned to the wild. She mated and gave birth to four different litters.

Shortly after her fourth litter, Pippa broke a shoulder in a fight. Joy took her to a veterinarian in Nairobi. But sadly in October 1969 Pippa died of heart failure.

That same year, something else terrible happened. Boy **mauled** the young son of Meru's game warden.

At first, officials of the Park told George that he had to shoot and kill Boy. They also wanted George to shoot Girl as well, even though she had nothing to do with the attack.

George convinced the Park officials that shooting the lions would bring a lot of bad publicity to the Park. It would be bad for tourism. Tourists brought a lot of money into the country.

The park warden finally agreed. But he said that both Joy and George had to shut down their camp. They could no longer rehabilitate animals in Meru. They could no longer conduct their research there.

Joy and George had not been getting along for quite a while. Joy didn't like the fact that George smoked and drank. Now, she blamed George for getting her thrown out of Meru National Park. She wanted a divorce.

George reluctantly agreed. "I was genuinely fond of Joy," he wrote in 1986, "and it was sad that our marriage should break up like this after twenty-six years."

In the end, they never went through with the divorce. But they did separate. Joy went to Elsamere, a home she had bought in

1966. It was on the shore of Navaisha Lake. George continued to hunt for a new home in Kenya.

Then, one day Park officials had an idea for George. Would he be interested in moving to Kora? Kora was a remote and isolated area on the Tana River, the largest river in Kenya.

George immediately agreed. It was the perfect place to raise his lions in peace.

Think About It

1. After Boy mauled a young child, the park warden wanted George to shoot Boy. How did George convince the warden to let Boy live?

2. Name three reasons why Joy was upset with George and wanted a divorce.

Chapter 7
The Murder of Joy Adamson

"Before the story of Elsa, lions were seen as big game to be hunted and killed by rich white hunters. After Born Free, *lions became wildlife to be protected and conserved."*

— Tony Fitzjohn

AT KORA, George and his brother Terence built a camp they called Kampi ya Simba (Camp of the Lions). It was a very basic camp. There was a **mess hut** and three sleeping huts. It was surrounded by a tall chain-link fence. The fence kept the wild animals out and the orphaned lions in.

Adamson at Kampi ya Simba.

George was enjoying his simple life there with his lions, including Boy and Girl. Then, one day in 1971 tragedy struck.

George was having breakfast in the mess tent. Suddenly he heard terrified screams from outside. It sounded like Stanley, George's assistant!

George rushed out. He saw Boy with Stanley in his jaws. George raised his rifle. He fired, killing Boy instantly.

He then rushed over to Stanley. But he was too late. Stanley had bled to death.

George was devastated. He was sad that he could not save Stanley. But he was also sad that he had to shoot his beloved Boy. He blamed himself.

The police took Stanley's body to a nearby town where he was buried. George and a camp worker buried Boy near the camp.

Meanwhile, during these years, friends noticed that Joy was beginning to change. She no longer wanted to spend time with friends. She just wanted to be with her wild animals.

Sadly, she also began making a lot of enemies. Some people said she treated her staff members as if they were her property. A former secretary said Joy no longer had any feelings for people.

Joy was now in her sixties. But she still had one big goal. What was that? She wanted to help an orphaned leopard return to the wild — just like she had done with Elsa, a lion, and with Pippa, a cheetah.

In 1976 a park ranger called Joy. He had exactly what she was looking for — a leopard cub! Would she be interested in taking it?

Joy jumped at the chance. She named the cub Penny.

Joy then moved her staff and Penny to a tented camp in Shaba National Reserve in northern Kenya. Shaba was a better place to raise a leopard. Joy would spend the last three years of her life there.

During that time, Joy succeeded at teaching Penny to hunt in her natural **habitat.** She helped Penny learn how to survive in the wild.

Joy was now 69 years old. But she still loved to spend the day in the bush with her animals. Usually, she would return to camp by 7 p.m. to listen to the news.

But on January 3, 1980, Joy did not return to her camp at the usual time. By 7:15 p.m. her employees became worried. They went to look for her. They found her body near the compound.

At first it was reported that Joy had been attacked and killed by a lion. But soon investigators decided she had been murdered. The injuries were caused by a sword-like weapon. But who would have done such a horrific thing? And why?

The police eventually arrested a man who worked for Joy. His name was Paul Nakware Ekai.

Ekai confessed to the murder. But later he recanted. He said he was forced to confess. He said he was tortured until he confessed.

Still, a court found him guilty. He was sent to prison. Twenty-four years later, in 2004, he spoke about the murder from his prison cell for the first time to a reporter.

Ekai disputed claims that Joy had died from stab wounds. He claimed he shot her for revenge. She had not paid him, he said, for his work at her camp.

But did Ekai really shoot Joy Adamson? If so, why did the police say she was stabbed? Perhaps we'll never know.

Think About It

1. The text says that Ekai "recanted" his confession. Based on the text, what does it mean to recant?

2. Write a newspaper article announcing the death of Joy Adamson. Tell about her accomplishments. Tell what she was like as she grew older.

A Day at Kamapi ya Simba

IMAGINE what it would be like not to have a cell phone. Or a computer. Or even a TV!

Life would be a lot different than it is today, right?

George Adamson didn't have any of those things at his camp at Kora in Kenya. So what was his life like at the camp? Let's pretend you're spending a day with George.

You wake up when the sun comes up and are greeted by your BFFs — a pride of lions that you've raised since they were born.

After a cup of tea, you walk the lions down to the river, three miles away. On your way, you pass by the beautiful Datura plant. Sometimes it's called angel's trumpets. That's because the plant has beautiful white trumpet-shaped flowers. But beware! It's beautiful, but poisonous. Eating any part of it can be deadly.

As you approach the river you hear baboons chattering in the trees. You see hippos wallowing and snorting in the water as the temperature hits 100 degrees.

At the river, you take a morning bath. Good thing you brought your assistant along. He stands guard with a rifle — just in case the crocodiles in river get a little extra hungry that morning.

Later, you return to camp for lunch. Goat meat today, same as yesterday. You then take a short siesta or nap before you greet some new visitors to the camp. They want to know everything about living in the African bush. They wonder if it is really dangerous. It is!

By evening you prepare meat for the pride's evening meal. Zebra meat this time. You also have your own dinner. You then check for messages. They are not text or e-mail messages. Rather, they are messages you get by short-wave radio — with lots of static.

You then write in your diary about your day before turning in for the night with a group lion cubs lying by our side.

It's just another day at Kampi ya Simba

Chapter 8
To Give Lions a Decent Life

"If you treat lions with respect, understanding, and love, they respond with their trust and affection."

— Tony Fitzjohn

JOY HAD ALWAYS SAID she wanted to be **cremated** when she died. She wanted her ashes to be placed with Elsa and Pippa. They were buried in the Meru National Park.

George honored Joy's wishes. He placed half of her ashes on Pippa's grave. He placed the other half on the grave of Joy's beloved Elsa.

Afterwards, George returned to Kampi ya Simba.

By now, another young man had been living and working at the camp for several years. His name was Tony Fitzjohn. Tony was like a son to George.

Together, George and Tony raised orphan lions. They reintroduced them into the wild. They watched them join a pride of other lions. They saw them produce offspring and live successfully in the African bush.

But living with lions is dangerous — even if they are lions that you've raised and loved. Over the years, many staff members and visitors were attacked; some were killed.

George's brother Terence was mauled badly by a lion once. So was Tony. He almost died. But, as he put it, it was a small price to pay "for the privilege of living with animals."

Tony Fitzjohn and his Bugsy.

One morning in 1977 George went out for a walk with one of his lions named Suleiman. George had raised and loved Suleiman from the time he was a year old.

Everything seemed fine. Then, suddenly, Suleiman jumped George from behind — for no reason! Suleiman sank his teeth into George's neck and held on. Blood gushed from George's neck.

Fortunately George had his revolver with him. He fired a shot over his shoulder. The bullet only grazed Suleiman. But it was enough to cause Suleiman to back off.

The staff at the camp heard the commotion and rushed out. They managed to get George to a hospital in Nairobi.

Somehow, he survived the terrible attack. Life went on as normal at Kora.

A few years later, in February 1989, George celebrated his 83rd birthday. He was now an old man. His eyesight was failing. Yet, overall, he was generally healthy and robust.

On August 20th of that year, George was expecting visitors. He heard their small plane land on the dirt airstrip not far away.

Another guest named Inge was already at the camp. She and an employee said they would go pick up the new guests in the Land Rover.

On their way to the airstrip, tragedy struck. They were **ambushed** by Somali **Shifta**. Three men with rifles opened fire on the Land Rover.

George heard the gunfire. Without hesitating, he and two of his workers jumped in another car. They headed toward the airstrip.

As he rounded a bend, George saw the bandits ahead of him. He stomped on the gas pedal! He drove directly toward the bandits.

They opened fire. One bullet hit George, killing him instantly. The two staff members were also killed. The bandits grabbed George's watch and gun and fled.

During the commotion, Inge and the employee slipped away. They hid in the bush until help arrived.

Later, Inge told the story of what happened. George Adamson had saved her life, she said.

George was buried in the Kora National Park. He was laid to rest near to his brother Terence, who had died a few years earlier, and his beloved lion friend Boy.

"There will never be another person like George Adamson," a friend said at George's funeral. "He devoted his life to helping wildlife and to protecting the unique environment in which they lived."

Once, George was asked by a visitor what he thought his purpose was at Kora. He thought for a moment. Then, he answered: "I suppose," he said, "it is to give the lions the chance of a decent life." No one ever did it better.

Think About It

1. The text says a bullet "grazed" the lion Suleiman. From what you've read, what can you conclude is the meaning of "graze" in this context?

2. What does the text say about living with lions? Give specific details from the text which support your conclusion.

Epilogue
Respect for the Animals

~~~~~~

Civilized man has spent untold treasure preserving ancient buildings and works of art fashioned by his own hand, yet he destroys these creatures of ageless beauty.

— George Adamson

~~~~~~

George Adamson and one of his lions.

For nearly 40 years, Joy and George Adamson risked their lives every day to protect the animals they loved so much. During that time, Joy often asked one simple question: Why do some men need to make an animal appear to be dangerous and aggressive? Is it to prove that they are better than the animal? Is it so they can brag about how they conquered a fierce jungle animal?

"I am sorry for people who cannot see an animal on its own merits," she often said, "and give [that animal] the same respect they want for themselves."

Perhaps that is the simple **legacy** of Joy and George Adamson. Together, they respected the animals. At the same time, they helped change the way people throughout the world think about wild animals and their place in the world. For that reason alone, Joy and George Adamson will always be remembered as wildlife heroes.

Think About It

1. The title of this book is *Wildlife Heroes*. Is this a good title? Why or why not? Write a different title for this book.

Timeline

1906 — George Adamson is born in India.

1910 — Friederike Victoria Gessner (Joy Adamson) is born in Austria on January 20.

1924 — George Adamson moves to Kenya. At the time, Kenya is still an English colony.

1935 — Joy marries first husband, known as Ziebel.

1938 — Joy marries her second husband, Peter Bally.

1938 — George joins Kenya's game department as a warden of the Northern Frontier District.

1944 — (January) Joy and George marry.

1947 — Joy begins a series of paintings to record tribal life and customs. The project takes six years and includes 700 portraits.

1956 — George kills a charging lioness while searching for a man-eating lion. He takes her three cubs back to the camp. Two of the cubs are sent to a zoo. But Joy keeps the third cub. She calls it Elsa.

1959 — Joy and George begin efforts to reintroduce Elsa into the wild.

1960 — Joy publishes a book called *Born Free*. It is hugely successful and is translated into 24 languages.

1961 — Elsa dies of tick fever and is buried in Meru National Park.

1961— (September): George retires as a game warden and focuses exclusively on his work with lions.

1963 — Joy founds the Elsa Conservation Trust, an organization committed to wildlife conservation.

1965 — George heads an effort to reintroduce three lions featured in the *Born Free* film into the wild.

1966 — Columbia Pictures releases the film *Born Free*. It becomes a box office hit all over the world.

1969 — The lion Boy attacks the son of a Kenya Game Warden. Although the child survives, the attack hurts the reputation of George's lion rehabilitation program.

1970 — George and Joy separate; George moves to Kora to continue the program of rehabilitating lions.

1971 — George's assistant, Stanley, is killed by Boy. George is forced to shoot Boy.

1976 — Joy moves to Shaba Game Reserve to raise Penny, a leopard cub.

1980 —Joy Adamson is killed in Kenya. At first, police believe she was attacked by a lion. Later, police prove that she was murdered by an angry employee.

1989 —George Adamson, aged 83, is shot dead by bandits in Kenya. He is buried next to his favorite lion, Boy, and his brother Terence.

Source Notes

Introductory Quotation

1. "Who will now care for...." George Adamson, *My Pride and Joy*. London: Collins Harvill, 1986. P. 295.

Prologue

1. "Joy and George together...." Tony Fitzjohn, *Born Wild: The Extraordinary Story of One Man's Passion for Africa*." New York: Crown Publishers, 2010. E-Book Edition.

Chapter 1

1. "I felt like a murderess...." Joy Adamson, "*The Searching Spirit*." London, Collins Harvill, 1978. Page 19.

2. "I decided I could not...." "15 Years After Elsa the Born Free Couple, Joy 7 George Adamson, Have Drifted Apart," *People*, October 1976.

3. "George was opening up...." Adamson, *The Searching Spirit*. P. 78.

Chapter 2

1. "No one better knew...." The Christian Science Monitor as quoted in George Adamson: Lion's Best Friend. http://www.fatheroflions.org/GeorgeAdamson_Information.html. (Retrieved 6/28/14)

Chapter 3

1. "A lion deserves to be free...." Adamson, *My Pride and Joy*. P. 20.

2. "Little did I know...." Adamson, *The Searching Spirit*. P. 162.

3. " ...weakling in size...." Joy Adamson, *Born Free: A Lioness of Two Worlds*. New York: Pantheon, 1960. P. 21.

4. "As long as she...." Adamson, *Born Free* .

Chapter 4

1. "Sitting there with Elsa...." Adamson, *Born Free*.

2. "She was overjoyed to see us...." Adamson, *Born Free.*

3. "It was her first experience...." Adamson, *Born Free*.

Chapter 5

1. "Reading about Elsa...." Adamson, *The Searching Spirit*. P. 166.

2. "Suddenly, she got up." "How Elsa Died: Pathetic Fight of Pet Lioness," Chicago Daily Tribune, February 11, 1961.

3. "With Elsa's death...." Adamson, *The Searching Spirit*. P. 165.

Chapter 6

1. "Animals give us something...." Kenneth G. Gehret, "From a Different World," *The Christian Science Monitor*, December 26, 1962.

2. "I was genuinely fond..." Adamson, *My Pride and Joy*. P. 171.

Chapter 7

1. "Before the story of Elsa...." Fitzjohn, *Born Wild: The Extraordinary Story of One Man's Passion for Africa*."

Chapter 8

1. "If you treat...." Fitzjohn, *Born Wild: The Extraordinary Story of One Man's Passion for Africa*."

2. "...for the privilege of living...." Fitzjohn, *Born Wild: The Extraordinary Story of One Man's Passion for Africa*." (E-Book Chapter 1)

3. "There will never be...." George Adamson: Lion's Best Friend. http://www.fatheroflions.org/GeorgeAdamson_Information.html. (Retrieved 6/28/14)

4. "I suppose it is to give...." Adamson, *My Pride and Joy*. P. 20.

Epilogue

1. "Civilized man has spent...." Adamson, *My Pride and Joy*. P. 40.

2. "I am sorry...." Gehret, "From a Different World."

Works Consulted

George Adamson, *My Pride and Joy*. London: Collins Harvill Press, 1986.

Joy Adamson, *Born Free: A Lioness of Two Worlds*. New York: Pantheon, 1960.

—, *The Searching Spirit*. London: Collins and Harvill Press, 1978.

Tony Fitzjohn, *Born Wild: The Extraordinary Story of One Man's Passion for Africa*, Crown Publishers, 2010.

Kenneth G. Gehret, "From a Different World," *The Christian Science Monitor*, December 1962.

"There's a Lioness at Our House," Boston Globe, 1961, reprinted from Born Free

Glossary

African bush: Generally, a large unsettled, undeveloped area.

Ambush (n.): A surprise attack from a hidden position.

Botanist: One who is trained in the classification and study of plants.

Carcass: A dead body, usually of an animal.

Conservationist: One who works to protect endangered plant and animal species and their habitats.

Cremate: To reduce a dead body to ashes by burning.

Gameskeeper: One who is employed to maintain and protect wildlife on private property.

Game warden: Someone whose job it is to enforce game laws, to prevent poaching, and to deal with wild animals that have attacked the tribesmen.

Habitat: The natural environment and home of a plant or animal.

Legacy: The lasting result of past events. *Joy and George Adamson's legacy is the wider protection of wild animals in Kenya.*

Maul: To injure, often by the clawing of wild animals.

Medicinal: Having to do with healing or curing an illness.

Mess hut: A place where food is served; also mess tent.

National Park: An area that is designated specifically for the protection of wildlife; no person is allowed to live or graze stock in a national park.

National Reserve: An area designated to protect wildlife, though the reasonable needs of people living within the area takes preference.

Natural born instinct: An unlearned behavior or characteristic; something a living organism is born with rather than acquires.

Poacher: One who illegally hunts, captures, and/or kills wild animals.

Predator: Among wildlife, an animal that lives by killing and eating other animals; also a person who kills or harms wild animals.

Preservation: To keep something in its original state.

Prey: (n.) An animal that is hunted or killed by another animal for food. *The lion stalked it prey.*

Pride: A group of lions.

Rehabilitate: To bring back or restore something to a previous or natural condition. *Joy and George Adamson rehabilitated orphaned lions to the wild.*

Safari: A trip to see or hunt animals, particularly in Africa.

Shifta: Armed gangs of bandits and poachers from Somali.

Photo Acknowledgments

About the Author

Jack L. Roberts is a freelance author who writes nonfiction books for young readers. His books include biographies of Nelson Mandela, Dian Fossey, Garth Brooks, Oskar Schindler, and many others. He is also the founder of publisher of Curious Kids Press (www.curiouskidspress.com), an educational publishing company focusing on nonfiction books for young readers. He resides in Palm Springs, California.